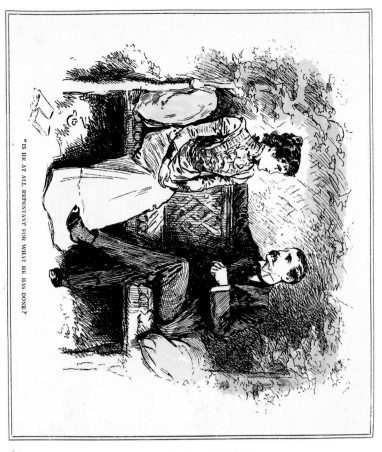

"IS HE AT ALL REPENTANT FOR WHAT HE HAS DONE?"

1

2

"In The Arbour"

4

5

3

1

"IS HE AT ALL REPENTANT FOR WHAT HE HAS DONE?"

2

"In The Arbour"

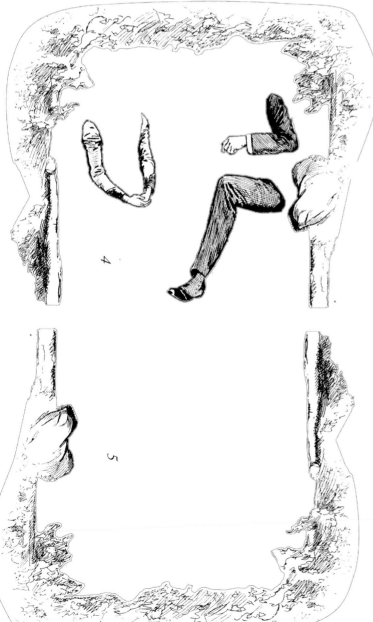

3

4

5

"FACT IS, WE'RE ENGAGED."

1

2

4

"We're Engaged"

3

5

"FACT IS, WE'RE ENGAGED."

1

3

"We're Engaged"

5

2

4

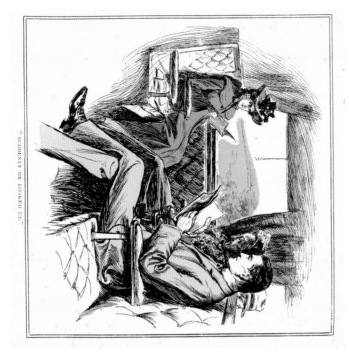

1

"SUDDENLY HE LOOKED UP."

3

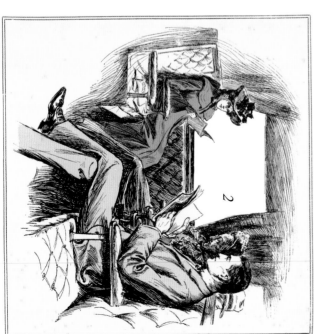

2

4

"Railway Carriage"

5

1

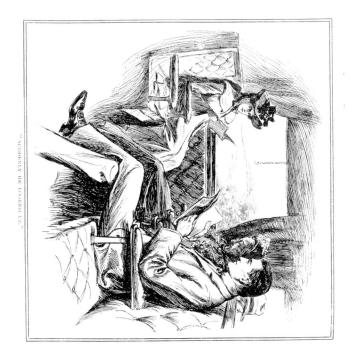

2

3

4

5

"Railway Carriage"

1

"A Happy Woman"

5

"I'M JUST AS HAPPY AS A WOMAN CAN BE"

3

2

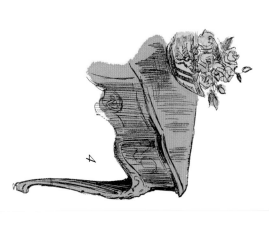

4

1

5

"I'M JUST AS HAPPY AS A WOMAN CAN BE."

"A Happy Woman"

3

2

4

ANNE BURST INTO A LOUD LAUGH.

1

2

4

"Anne Laughed"

3

ANNE BURST INTO A LOUD LAUGH.

4

"Anne Laughed"

2

3

1

4

5

"Bedside Confrontation"

2

3

6

1

4

5

"Bedside Confrontation"

2

3

6

2

4

3

1

5

"Schoolroom"

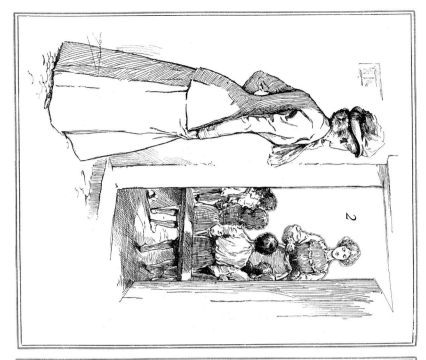

"Schoolroom"

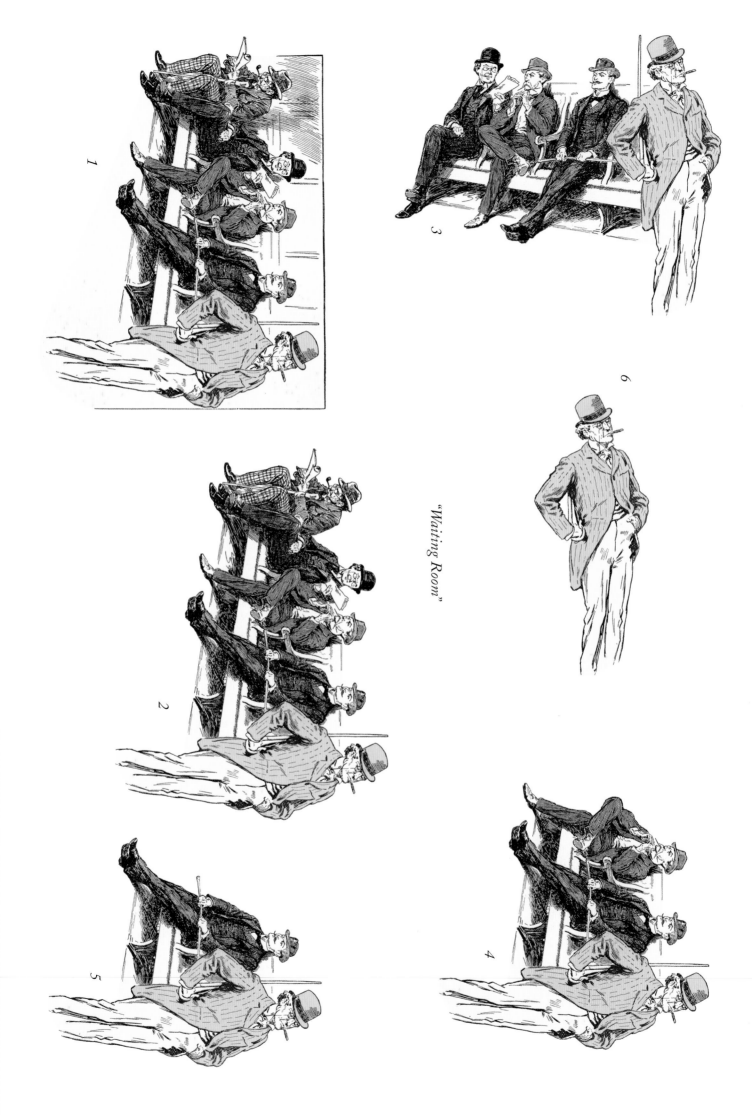

"Waiting Room"

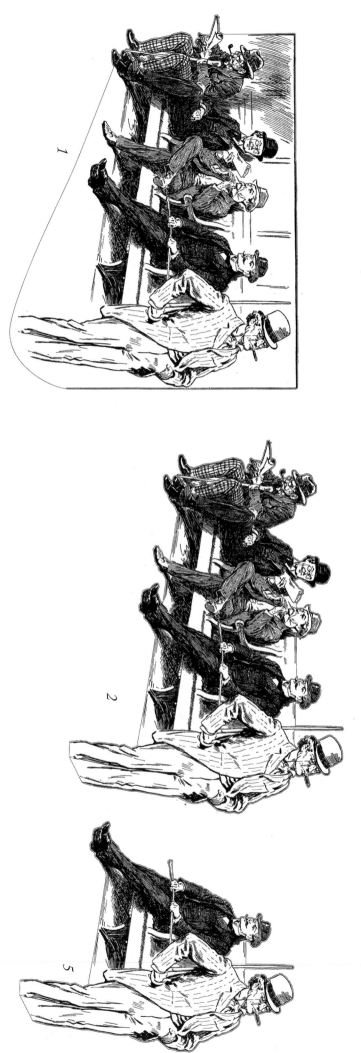

"Waiting Room"